Georg Keilhofer's Traditional Carving Techniques

Scenic Relief Carving

Schiffer Publishing Ltd

77 Lower Valley Road, Atglen, PA 19310

Georg Keilhofer

Text written with and photography by Douglas Congdon-Martin

Dedication

To everyone who is beginning to learn the art of woodcarving

Printed in Hong Kong

ISBN: 0-88740-788-9

Book Design by Audrey L. Whiteside.

Library of Congress Cataloging-in-Publication Data

Keilhofer, Georg.
　　Scenic relief carving/Georg Keilhofer; text written with and photography by Douglas Congdon-Martin.
　　　　p.　　cm. -- (Georg Keilhofer's traditional carving)
　　　　ISBN 0-88740-788-9
　　1. Wood-carving--Technique. 2. Relief (Decorative arts) 3. Landscape in art.　I. Congdon-Martin, Douglas.　II. Title.　III. Series: Keilhofer, Georg. Georg Keilhofer's traditional carving.
　　TT199.7.K453　　1996
　　731.4'62--dc20　　　　　　　　　　　　　　95-26285
　　　　　　　　　　　　　　　　　　　　　　　　　CIP

Published by Schiffer Publishing, Ltd.
77 Lower Valley Road
Atglen, PA 19310
Please write for a free catalog.
This book may be purchased from the publisher.
Please include $2.95 postage.
Try your bookstore first.

We are interested in hearing from authors
with book ideas on related subjects.

Contents

Introduction

Beginning carvers often encounter frustration with both tools and wood. This book, the second I have written for novice carvers, is a valuable continuation of the learning process, especially how to choose and use the correct tools and how to read the grain in different types of wood.

One lesson you will learn right away is the importance of using a high quality wood. Cheaper woods are often grainy and do not allow you to carve the details you are after. This especially true if your tools are less than super sharp. Sharp tools go where you want them to and cut cleanly and crisply. When you carve this way there is never a need for sandpaper. In fact, when I teach, I emphasize that my students not use sandpaper, because it will ruin the fresh appearance of a tool cut.

Finally, I strongly suggest that you spend some time studying the anatomy of the animals you are carving. The kind of carving I do is realistic so the importance of anatomy is clear, but even caricature carvers have to pay attention to anatomy if their carvings are to be recognizable.

This book follows the same course of instruction I use with classes in my studio. As I tell students, when the basics are learned, all that is necessary to prevail is persistance and patience. Enjoy!

If you have interest in persuing a class in carving, write for a schedule of classes to the Frankenmuth Woodcarving Studio, 976 South Main Street, Frankenmuth, Michigan 48734.

The Project Pattern

This pattern is 77% of original size.

The Relief Carving

The project is carved on a board measuring 11" x 13-1/2" with a thickness of 1-3/8".

Align the pattern over the carbon paper and tape in place.

Lay a piece of carbon or tracing paper on the wood, carbon side down.

Go over the lines with a pencil to transfer the pattern to the wood.

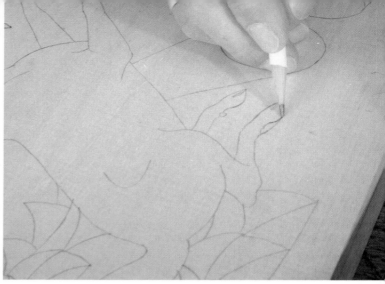

Draw a line on the side. It starts 1/4" from the front surface at the bottom of the piece, and tapers to 1/2" about 5" up the edge. The line continues from there to the top at 1/2". the background will be removed to this line and the taper will give dimensionality to the work.

Do the same at the back of the hooves.

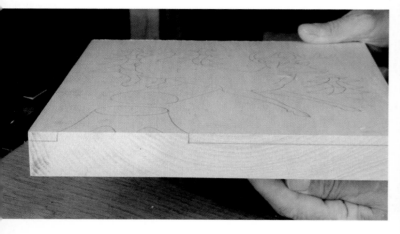

The line continues across the bottom edge, 1/4" from the front surface. It is interrupted at the borders of the stump.

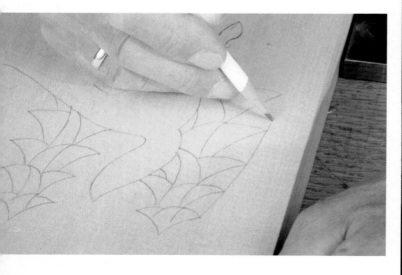

Connect the points of the trees and the antlers. When roughing I will stop at this line so I don't damage the detailed areas.

Ready for rough carving.

I use a mallet to drive the chisel during the removal of excess wood. The mallet is safer than pressing by hand. If you hit it lightly it makes a short cut; if you hit it harder it goes further. This control is very useful in the aggressive removal process. Choose a mallet that is comfortable for you in size and weight. The chisels for removing excess are #4/18mm, #6/18mm, and #39/8mm.

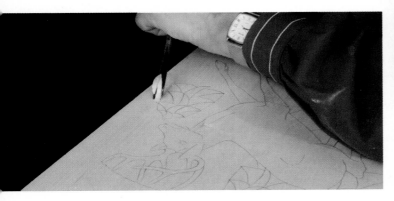

I begin with #39/8mm v-tool. With this I follow the outside lines of the figures.

You must be aware of grain direction. You should always try to carve from shorter grain to longer grain. This means I come up the face but down the front of the antlers.

When using the v-tool, I keep the edge that is following the pattern almost perpendicular. I have to be careful not to let the other corner be pulled too deeply into the wood, but, because the background is going to be removed, I don't need to worry much about tearing.

Continue around the outline of the figures.

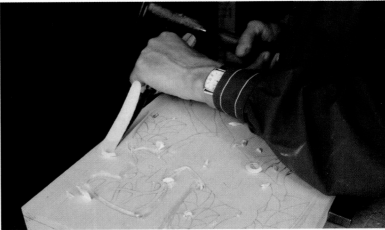

When the outline is established, I switch to a #6/18mm to remove the background. I use the #6/18mm because the corners curve up to cut the fibers and allow me to go deeper without unwanted damage. A flat chisel does not cut the fibers and can cause uncontrolled breakage of wood.

I am running into grain here, causing the tearing. Because I am going quite deep here, it doesn't concern me. If I didn't have so much wood to work with, I would switch directions to get a smoother, safer cut.

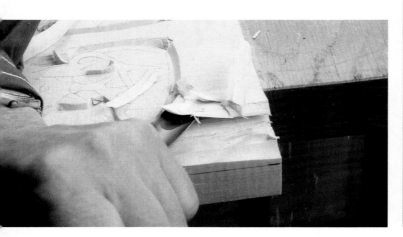

On the cross grain cut I bury the right corner of the chisel and keep the left corner raised. This lifts the wood and saves a lot of work.

Continue across the top.

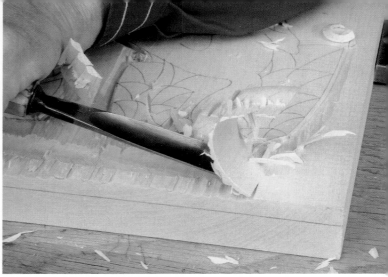

You should not go deeper than the v-tool cut outline. If you do you may split the figure.

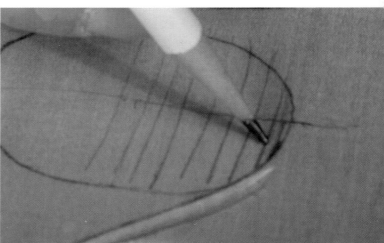

To determine the direction of the cut relative to the grain it is helpful to do some drawing. A line running perpendicular to the grain at the widest point of a curve is the reference line. Other lines, representing the direction of the grain, are drawn across the center line..

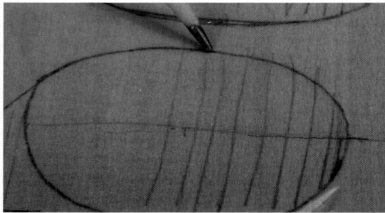

You can see that the grain gets longer as you move away from the center line this way...

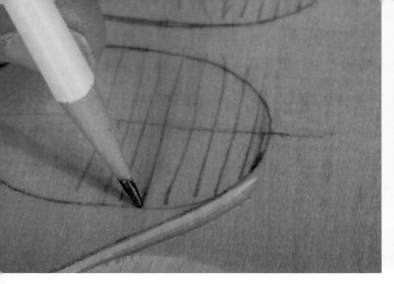

and this.

Cut in the direction of the arrows stopping where the grain shifts...

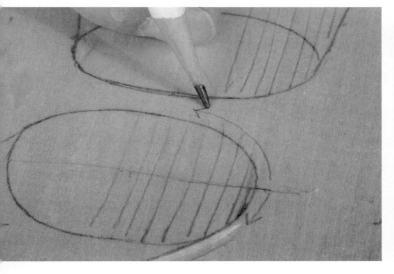

The direction of the cut should move away from the center, going from shorter grain to longer grain.

and coming at it from the other direction.

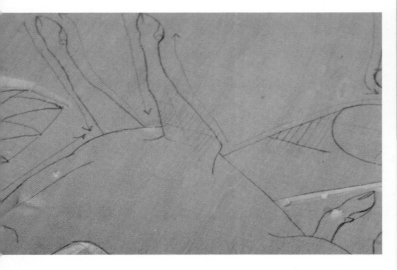

The method works with all lines going at an angle across grain, and, until your eye is used to seeing it, you will find it helpful to draw the directions of the cut.

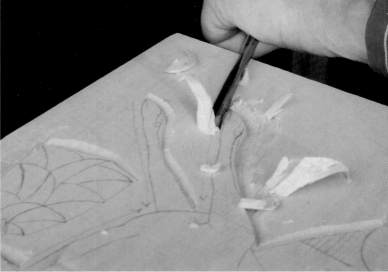

If I find that the grain is carrying the tool into the wood, I break it off...

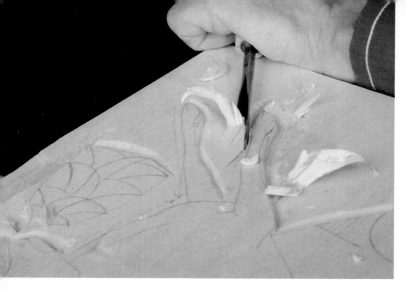

and start anew, a little shallower.

switch directions and cut down the front edge of the deer's neck, creating a stop and avoiding damage. You must stay aware as you carve and be able to stop right away.

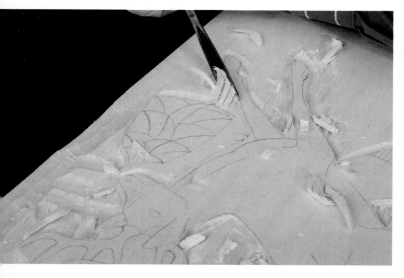

Because the bottom edge of the tree has already been outlined, I can come aggressively up the front of the leg. The outline of the tree acts as a stop, protecting it from unintended damage.

Continue to remove the background.

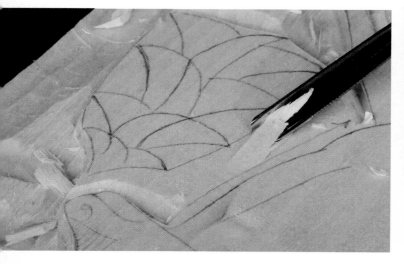

Coming up the side of the tree the wood begins to break toward the neck of the deer, so I stop immediately...

When the first level of background is removed, we need to return to the #39/8mm v-tool and deepen the outlines.

For the next stage of background removal I switch to a #4/18mm. This has less of a sweep, so it doesn't cut as deeply as the #6/18mm.

You want the background to be level. Avoid the tendency to have it slope up to the edge of the figure.

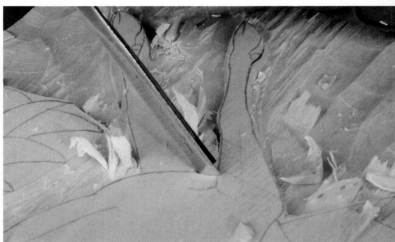

Use the v-tool to clean up the area at the top of the front legs. Use one side of the v-tool to cut shallowly along the chest line taking the cut to the other leg.

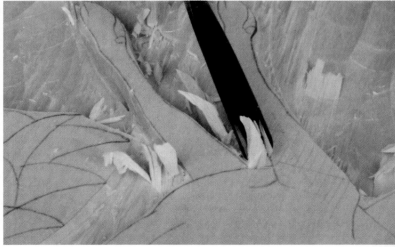

With the #4/18mm we want to go down about 1/16" above the final depth, leaving room to finish the background.

Trim back along the front edge of the leg to the stop you created.

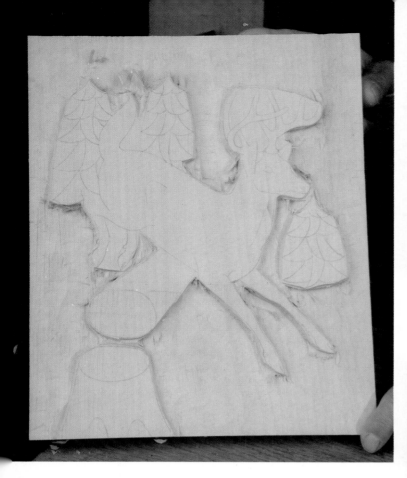

Continue to remove the excess wood from the background to this point.

Here you can see a new blade compared to the ground blade. The crown of the cutting edge lifts the corners, keeping them off the background. This provides a margin of safety.

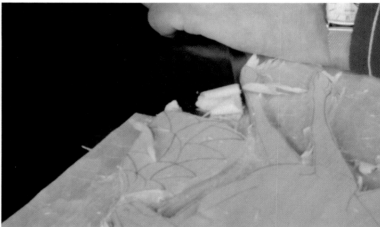

While this is a wide tool, you can use just a portion of the edge in smaller areas, still giving a nice even cut.

I use a #1/70mm Swiss shave tool to even-up the background. It is a straight cutting edge, but has a crown to the edge which lifts the corners.

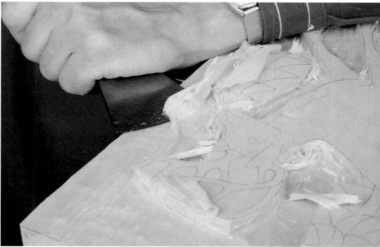

In large areas the tool is used in a slicing cut, coming across the direction of the grain. If you meet resistance, change the direction of the cut.

When going cross grain, keep the tool angled to slice. If you run against the grain, like I have here...

Set a depth gauge by laying a straight edge across the figure and measuring to the line you drew on the side. Remember the line tapers up at the bottom of the board. Make sure you have the correct depth for the area you are checking.

change the angle of the tool and continue in the same direction.

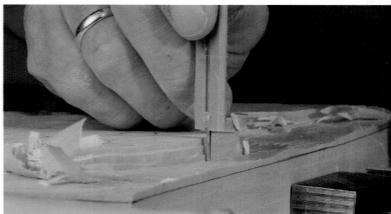

The gap between the gauge and the surface shows how much background you need to remove.

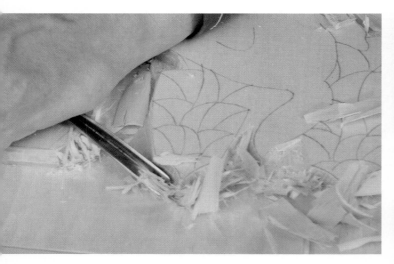

Use the v-tool to clean up the shavings around the figures. I don't want to cut straight down with a gouge here, because I may cut too deeply into the background.

Here we have almost reached the final depth.

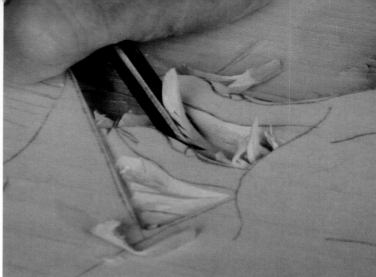

To use this wide tool in a narrow spot, I hold my finger on the under side of the blade, running it against the edge of the wood. This gives me the control I need.

In an area like this, between the back legs, I use a v-tool as long as I have room...

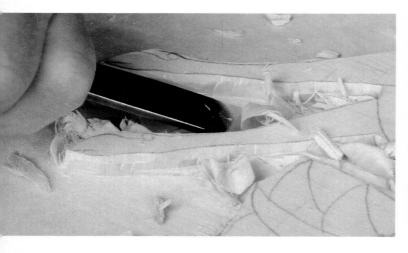

In small, tight areas you can switch to a smaller tool. This is a #2 1/2/18mm chisel.

then I switch to chisels. This is a #2-1/2/18mm, used for the straight portion.

On the edges of the figures there will be some areas where you can't use the v-tool. Use a #2-1/2/18mm or another chisel and cut straight down. Work gently and be careful not to cut into the background.

When the leg segment is curved I switch to #4/10mm, matching the curve. With the chisel's bevel vertical, I push straight down.

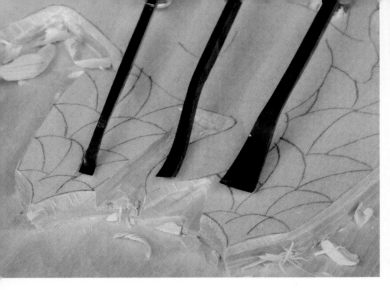

I need three sizes of short-bent chisels to get into some spots. They are #21/12mm, #21/6mm, and a #21/4mm with a custom-made shorter hook.

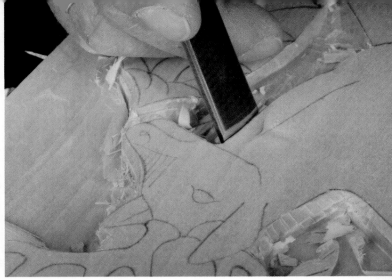

A #2-1/2/18mm is also helpful on the neck.

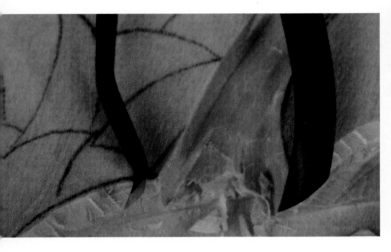

Here you can see how much more the chisel on the left is hooked. This allows it to get into tighter areas.

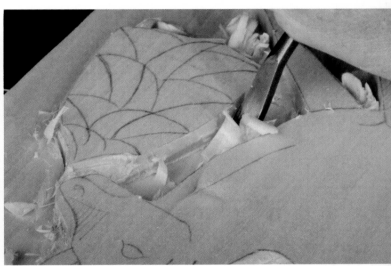

The short-bent chisels get into tight spaces to take the background to the proper level. This is the #21/12mm.

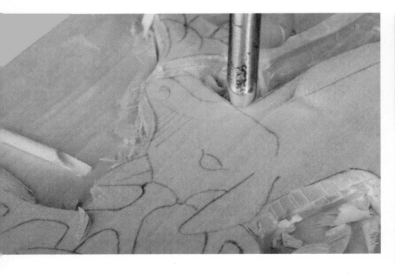

I will also use other tools like this #11/6mm gouge to cut the juncture of the head and neck. When using these tools remember: don't cut into the background.

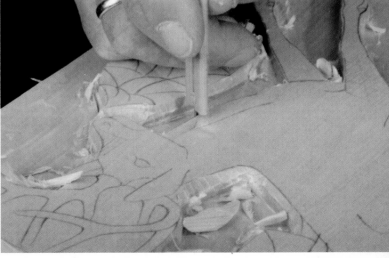

In these surrounded spaces it is necessary to use the depth gauge to assure the proper depth.

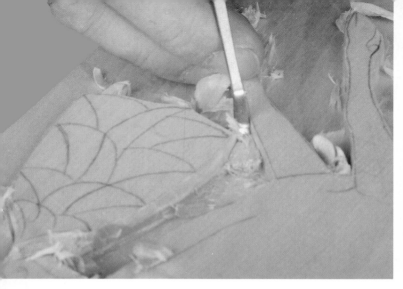

In this very narrow area the #21/4mm hook does the trick.

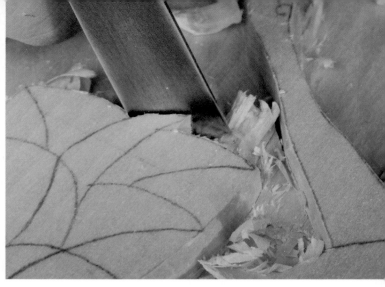

When using this wider tool, I lift up the outside corner so it doesn't cut into the background.

The v-tool pushed straight down with the bevel held vertically, starts to shape the bottom of the tree.

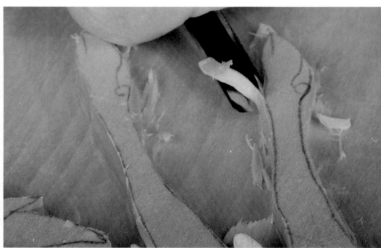

The v-tool can also be used to shape the legs without a straight cut-off. The legs are going to be undercut, and a straight cut would show. The first cut with the v-tool takes the top edge to the line.

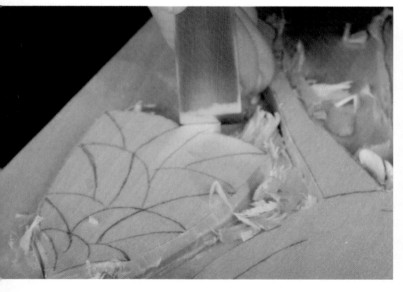

I clean up the bottom with a #4/18mm.

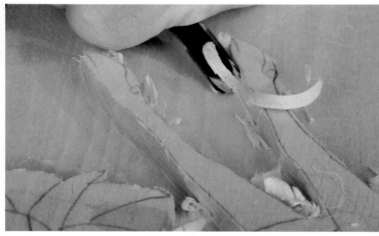

A second, lower cut brings the lower edge of the leg into shape.

16

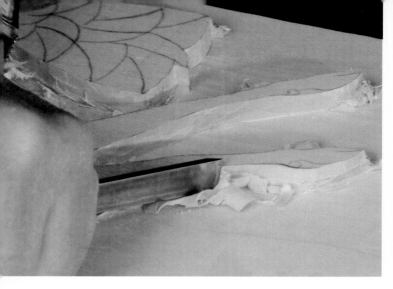

You can do the same thing with a #1/12mm chisel, which is wide enough to trim the edge in one cut. Hold the blade at an angle so it slices, letting the corner ride on the background without cutting deeply.

Clean up the area with the short bent. These spots are done one level at a time until you reach the desired depth. Recut the edges of the figures as you go.

You can use the same sliding cut on the edge of the log with a #1/18mm. Because the log is not to be undercut, it matters less if you cut into the background a little.

You can use the short-bent to pry away the excess wood at the end of a cut.

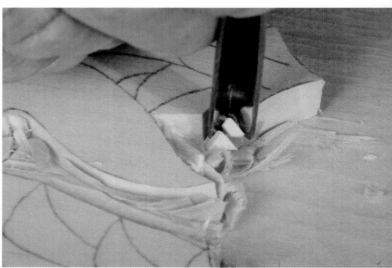

A small skew can be used to open narrow passages like this.

Working here I need to use the v-tool. This removes wood without putting too much pressure on the tree branch.

Cut on the underside of the bough first, going in about 1/16".

The point of the bough was a little bit torn, so I clean and flatten it with a #4/18mm chisel.

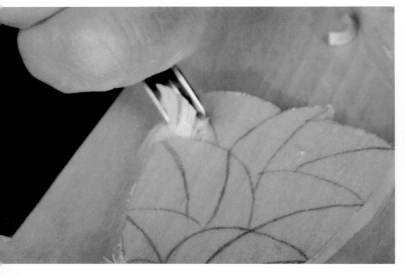

Next cut along the top of the bough. The pressure is on the wood that is to be removed, not on the branch.

With the waste removed, I can trim up the bough with a #4/18mm. The bevel is perpendicular, but the tool is angled back to give me a sliding cut.

Repeat the process until you get to the level of the background.

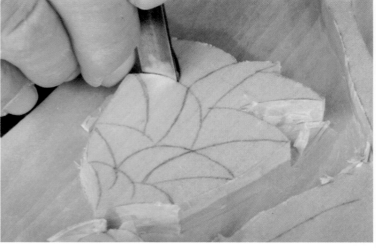

A #4/10mm chisel is used to cut the underside of the bough, going straight down to the background, if possible.

A v-tool cleans up most of the shavings.

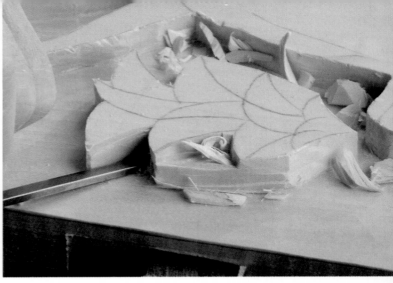

The #2/4mm skew cleans the background into the crotch of the branch.

A #1/12mm chisel cleans up the edge of the bough, going into the corner. Do the underside first...

Repeat the process on each bough.

then do the top of the lower bough.

Because of limited access on this side I use the short-bent chisels, first the large one...

19

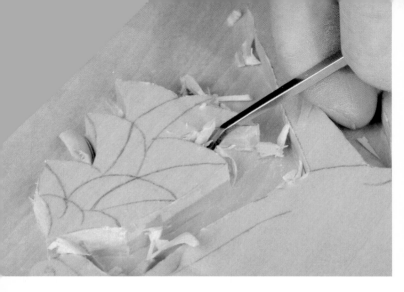

then a smaller one.

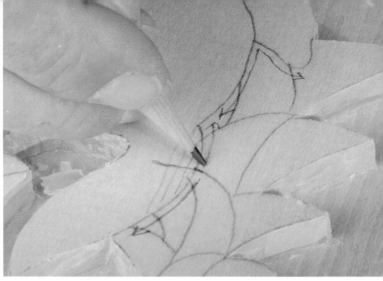

Determine the direction of the cuts at the hip, so they move from short grain to long grain.

To clean up the carving a cut straight down in the corner with the #2/4mm skew.

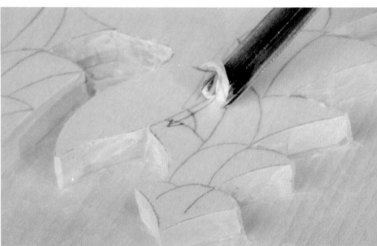

Tilt the v-tool so the edge following the line is almost vertical. Cut from short grain to long grain to establish the line of the hip and tail.

Then I turn the tool over and cut over the edge back into the corner. The skew is the only chisel that can accomplish this.

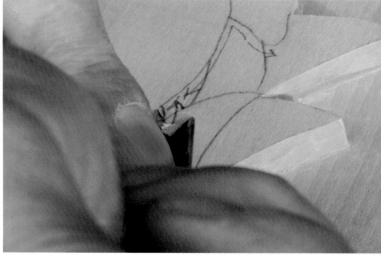

Where the grain shifts, shift direction.

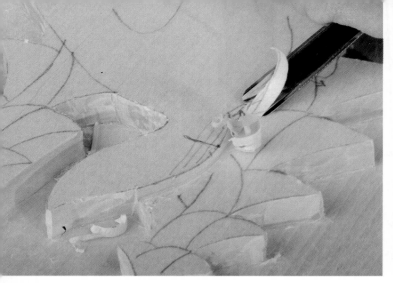

Come from the intersection of the hip and leg up to the tail...

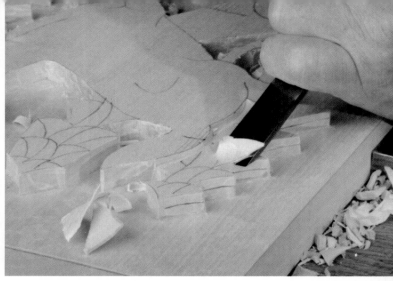

With a #1/18mm reduce the thickness of the tree to the level drawn. This may take several steps. Don't go deeper than the outline of the deer that you have already cut.

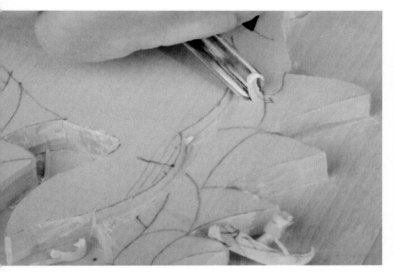

and, from the same intersection, cut around the joint of the leg.

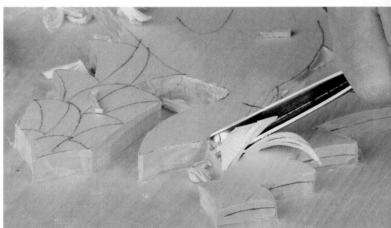

Reestablish the outline of the deer, making it deeper. This time I try to go down to the final level of the tree.

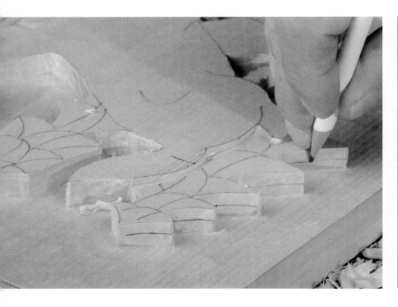

Mark the midline on the edge of the trees.

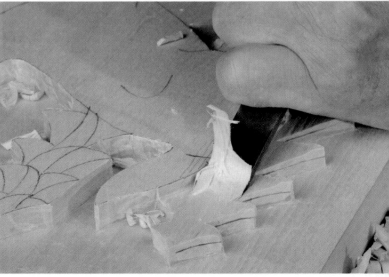

Continue relieving the surface of the tree.

With the corner of the #1/12mm chisel cut a deeper stop around the tail.

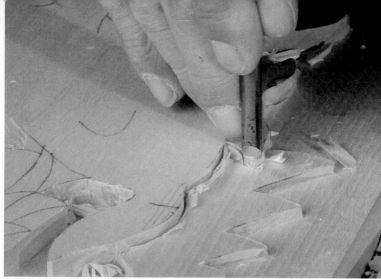

and with a #4/8mm cut down around the knee joint.

Do the same around the hip using a #2-1/2/18mm chisel.

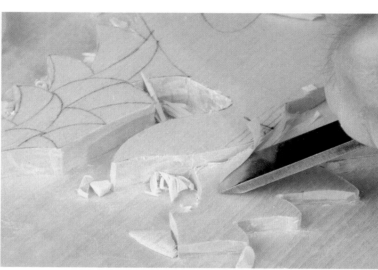

With a #1/18mm work from the center of the tree and round it into the cuts just made.

With a #4/10mm cut down on the line of the leg...

Do the same on the other side. It can be rounded pretty close to the background.

Taper the top of the tree with the #1/18mm.

Extend the lines of the antler so it connects to the other. Carving around this will keep it stable and whole until you are ready to carve it.

Carve out the four inner openings of the antlers, cutting until you are almost to the depth of the background. I do these openings first because the solid mass around them will support the carving.

With the centers of the openings carved away, you can start to clean up the edges by cutting straight down with a #1/6mm chisel. You don't want to undercut yet.

The #11/4mm cutting straight down conforms to the sharp corner...

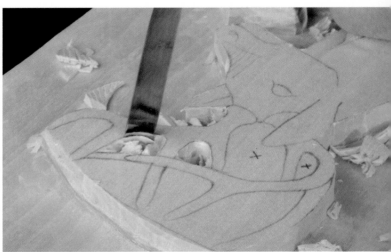

and the #6/8mm follows the curve of the lower edge. Use the chisel that fits the curve you are working on, but be sure to cut straight down.

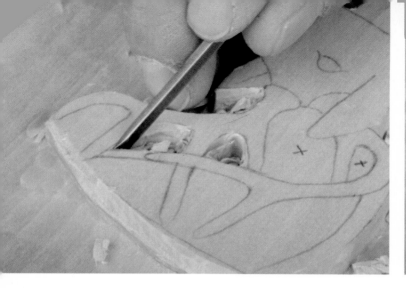

The skew is used to clean up the corner, as we did on the crotch of the tree.

In the larger opening you can make use of the v-tool.

The #21/4mm hooked short-bent reaches in to clean out the waste.

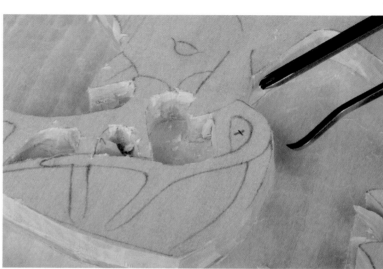

To clean the smallest hole I am using a #11/2 veiner and a #21/2 short-bent hook.

Check your progress with the depth gauge. The back antler will be cut pretty low, so this opening needs to go down to the background.

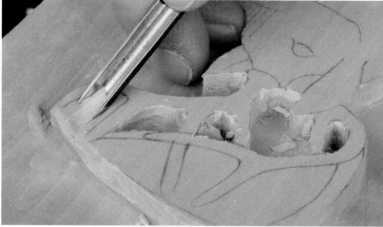

With the inner openings cleaned out, we can work on the outer openings in the antlers. I use a #11/6 to cut relieve the major area. The gouge cuts without creating much outward pressure that would break the antler.

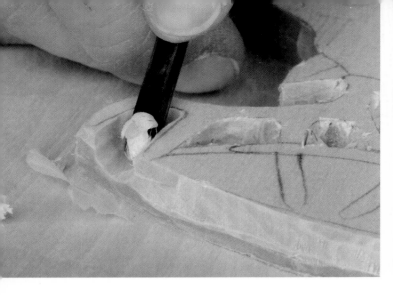

When I get lower I switch to a #11/4mm. Take small bites and don't pry with the tool. You will weaken the antler if you do.

The next opening is large enough that I can use my v-tool to remove the excess wood.

When the center is clear I can define the edges more. Here I cut straight down, moving my tool back and forth to help it cut.

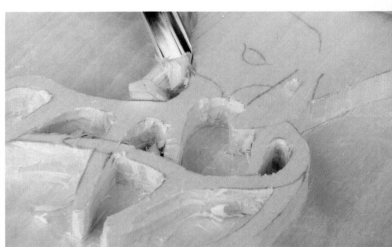

Cut the back ear down more than halfway.

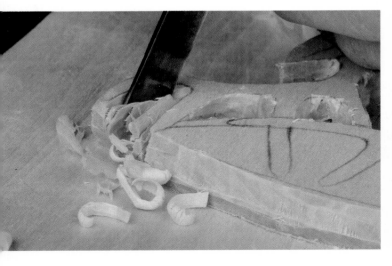

I use a variety of tools here as I did before, but I need to be especially careful of the fragile antler.

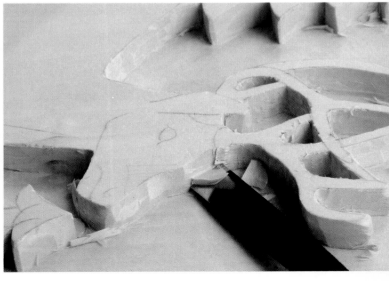

Taper the tip and the front edge of the back ear almost to the background.

Outline the base of the antler with the v-tool using the pencil line as the center.

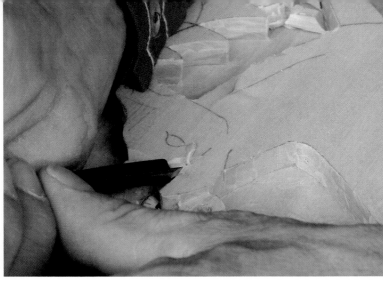

Continue outlining the antler where it goes behind the ear.

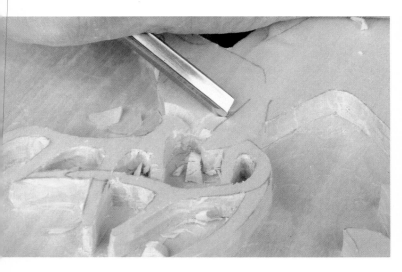

The line of the forward antler is done in the same way, but not as deeply.

Chamfer the front of the face at about a 30 degree angle.

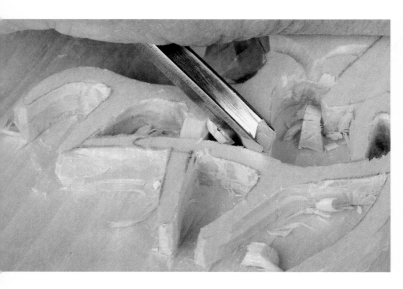

Outline the forward antler, carefully taking away from the back antler.

Slightly taper the front of the nose.

Open up the bridge between the front and back antler. I start the removal using the v-tool, and use other tools to cut straight down.

This is the kind of breakage that can occur when you slip. Fortunately it can be repaired with a little glue, after the antler is roughed in.

With the #4/18mm I reduce the back antler. The main antler goes down to about 1/8" thickness, while the points remain a little thicker. Start at the tips.

The forward antler has more than one depth. This back branch is at almost the same depth as the back antler, about 1/8". Reduce it in the same way.

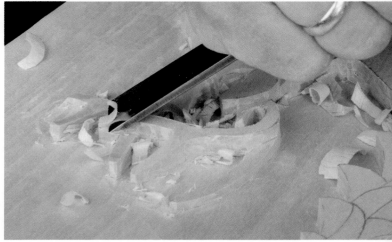

Next come up the main stem of the antler, being careful not to slip.

The forward antler stays pretty full at the top, being rounded to about half its current thickness.

With the antlers roughed in I can glue the broken piece in place. I use white glue.

Clean the shavings at the body with the v-tool.

The two legs that are in the background will be reduced about half way. First I mark their new thickness...

Do the same at the hind leg.

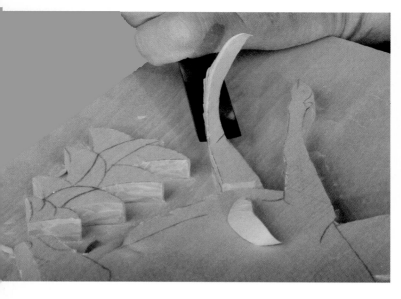

then I reduce with a #1/18mm.

Mark the log and stump for carving. Begin by drawing a line on the log, parallel to the body and touching the oval end of the trunk. Drawing a similar line on the stump, parallel to the ground. The log tapers from this line to the body at about half its thickness, and to the end of the cut at level of the ground. The cut end of the stump tapers from the ground at the top to the surface at the line.

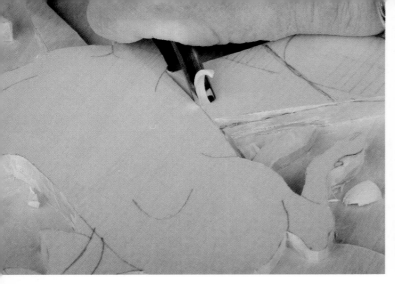

At the body, cut an outline with the v-tool.

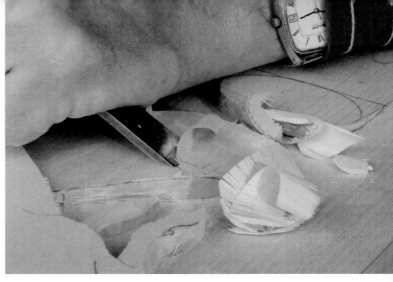

Do the same on the end of the log.

Taper the log back to the body using a #1/70mm or...

Repeat on the stump, cutting across the grain until you reach the line.

or a #1/18mm.

Redraw the oval of the log end.

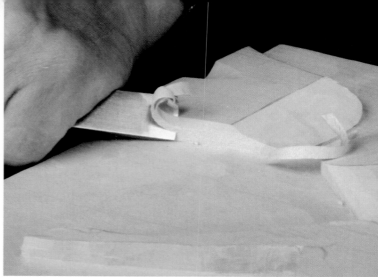

Use the #1/18mm, flat side down, to round off the log down to the oval.

Round off the corner of the stump with the #1/18mm. First take a little cut to set the angle.

The grain requires that you come down the log in opposite direction.

Then round toward the middle and the background.

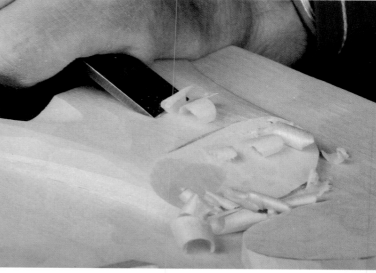

Use a #6/14mm to open the space between the roots in the stump.

I want to give the stump some contour, taking away the straightness and bringing out the root and top.

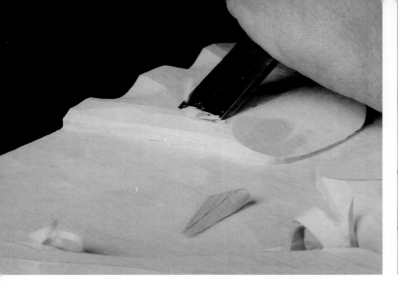

With a #2 1/2/18mm come across the stump to round it off.

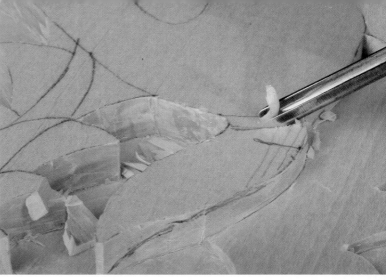

Come across the hip line with an #11/4mm.

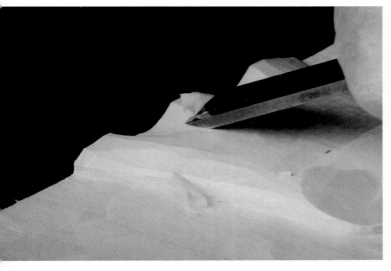

Round the roots.

Taper the tail to the hip line.

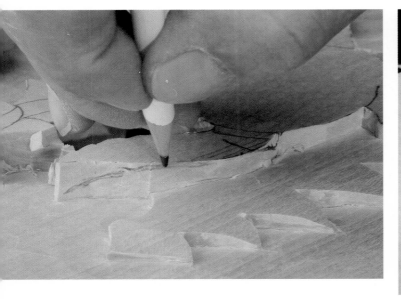

Returning to the deer, draw the line of the hip at the base of the tail and the curve of the tail.

and to the end. Keep the surface flat.

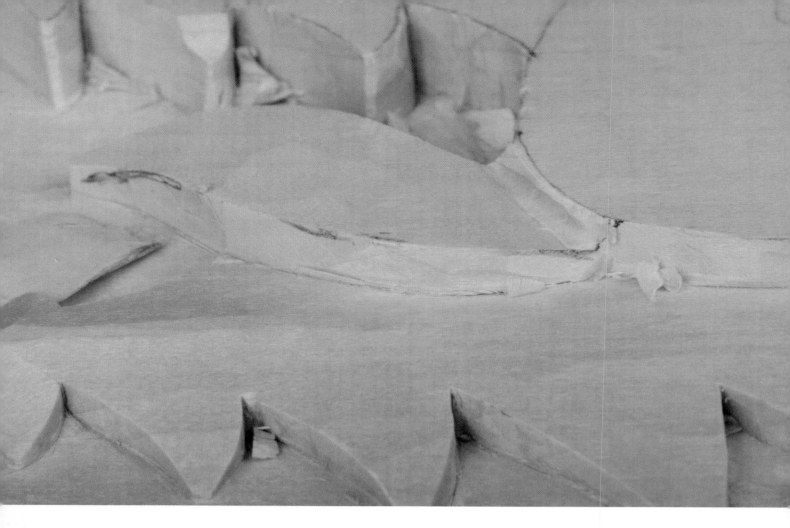

The result.

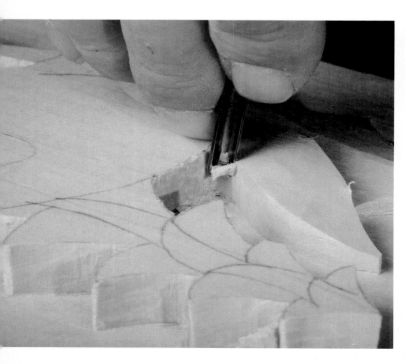

Round the tail down to the background. Begin at the base with a #11/4.

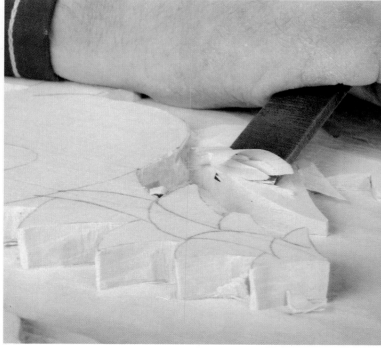

Continue rounding with the #1/18mm, flat side down.

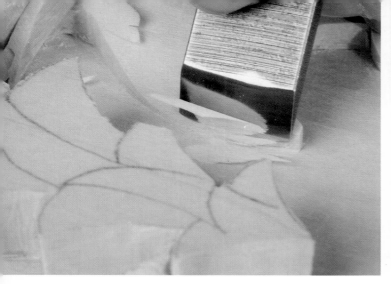

Carve down to the background in the front, but leave the back of the tail high.

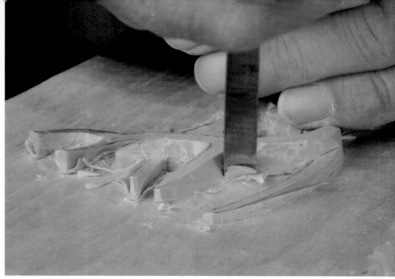

Go in about 1/16", not more.

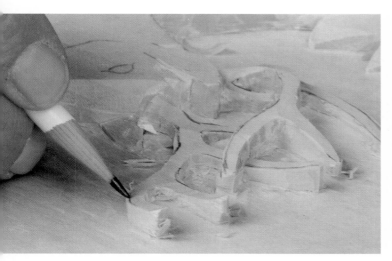

Redraw and size the antlers.

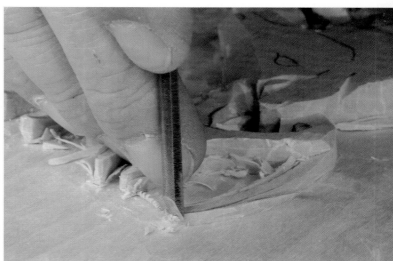

The #4/4mm will round off the points a little more.

Trim to the line, then, halfway down, undercut the antlers slightly. This will make them look thinner.

Continue undercutting at the back of the head.

When the undercutting is complete, clean up the background. Use a tool that works, which for me, is generally a short bent chisel. The corner of the tool will clean around the edge.

A skew is helpful for removing shavings.

Round off the antlers, following the short grain-to-long grain rule.

In the tighter curves I use a rounder tool like this #11/4mm. I come over the top and cut down, ending with a slight undercut.

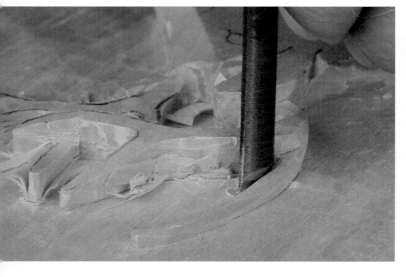

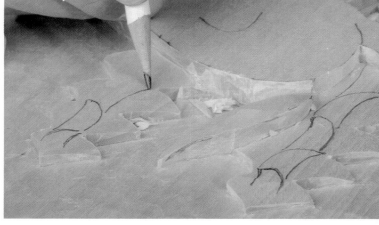

You may need to cut across the grain in some place to get a clean cut.

Redraw the boughs of the trees. You can refer to the pattern or freehand it, as I am. The top of one should pretty much line up with the bottom of the one below it.

The concave, inside curve is cut up, using the v-tool, following the pencil line.

Taper the point and the top down to the background.

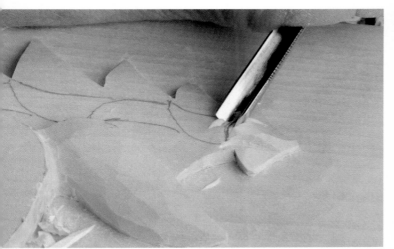

The convex, outside curve is cut down.

Both sides of the middle bough are tapered back to the v-cut.

Trim the surface of the outside boughs to the bottom of the v-cut. Use a #4/10mm the small branches and a #4/18mm for the large.

Use the #4/10mm chisel to carry the bottom line of the bough back to the center. This will act as a stop cut for the next level.

Repeat the process at the next level.

This little corner behind the tail has to be popped out to define the bough.

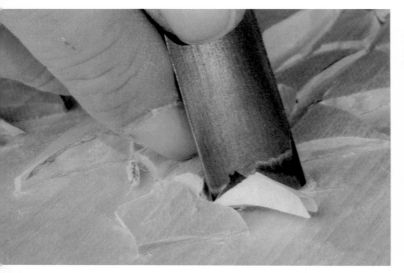

Taper the top edge and tip of the bough.

In the tighter areas you may need to use a #21/4mm short bent.

Bring the center bough into the groove and taper the sides into the v-cuts.

In this tight spot I need to use a #21/2mm short bent.

To texturize the smaller branches I use a #4/10mm chisel. I align it with the edge of the bough. Then, holding the tool at about a 30 degree angle, I move it back toward the center and walk it toward the edge.

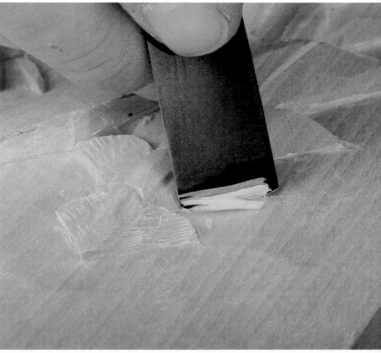

On the larger boughs I use a #4/18mm and do the same thing.

This leaves a lined pattern in the wood. Move the blade up and repeat.

The walking of the tool across the wood gives this pattern.

On the center bough I do the same thing, then with sliding cut, create some contour.

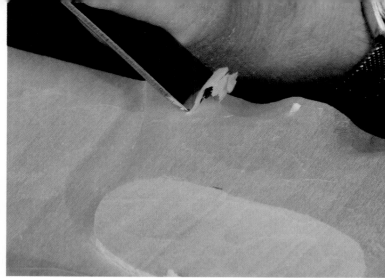

The same technique is used to create the texture of the bark of the stump and log. Start near the edge and work across...

and up. This texturing will be a little coarser than the tree boughs.

The result.

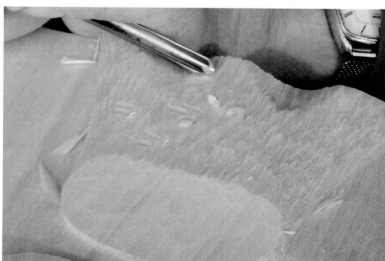

I add a few cuts with a #11/4mm to give it more character. Do not make them too even.

If the texturing is too even we can go over it with a #4/18mm chisel.

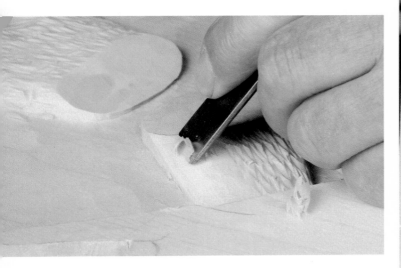

Repeat on the log.

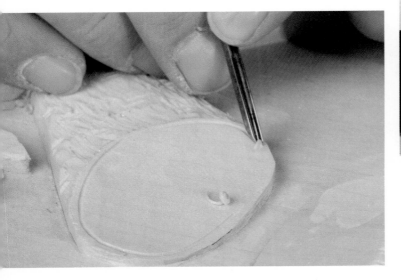

To finish the log I use a #11/1 veiner to create growth rings. This tool needs to be very sharp or, when cutting across the grain, you may split the growth rings.

Progress. The hill is drawn in from the upper middle left to the lower middle right.

The grass is made with a little different type of walking. Using a #4/18 I hold the front of the tool at about 45 degrees. I start straight...

twist it to the right...

twist the blade to the right...

and slide it off to the right. This pattern will cascade up as it moves, though this will not be noticeable when it covers the whole grassy area. The secret is to move the tool quickly, take small cuts, and get it out after the third or fourth cut.

straighten the blade...

In some places you may need to use the technique left-handed. This may take some practice.

Ready to begin the body.

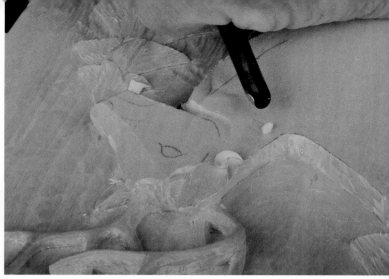

The shaping begins with a #11/6mm.

Outline the head.

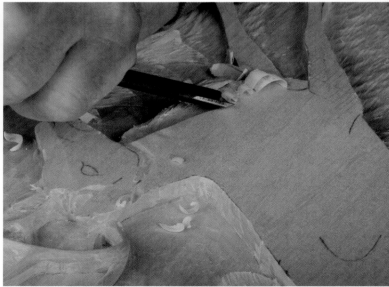

Shape the chest area using a #6/14mm.

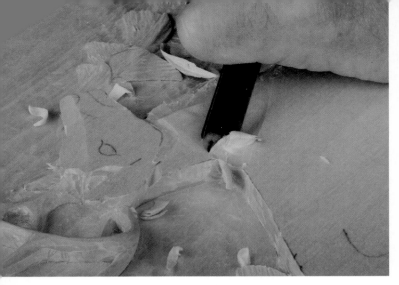

Switch to a #6/14mm to define the line of the shoulder.

Define the front edge of the upper leg going around it with the #11/6mm.

Round the back of the neck. I am using a #1/12mm.

With the #6/14mm carry the line of the back of the leg up to the shoulder.

With the cup away from the wood, soften the groove in the front of the neck and chest area.

With the #1/12mm shape the shoulder area.

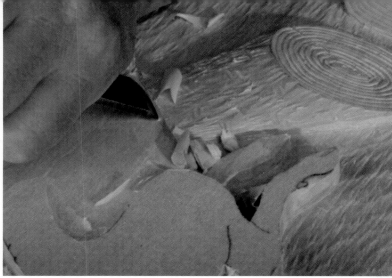

With a #6/14mm make cuts to indicate the bend of the hind leg. This is a difficult cut...

Round the bottom of the body, with the sole of the chisel against the body.

so come at it from both directions.

With the same tool, sole out, round the back.

Use a #1/18mm to shape the body up to that point.

Continue back to the tail.

With the #39/8 v-tool cut the fold in the hind leg, where it meets the hip.

The result.

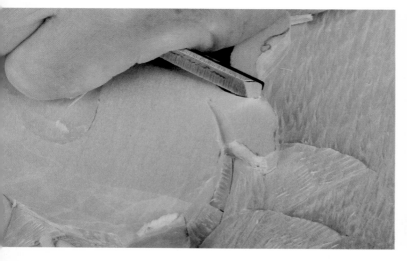

Use the same tool to come across the inside of the knee joint.

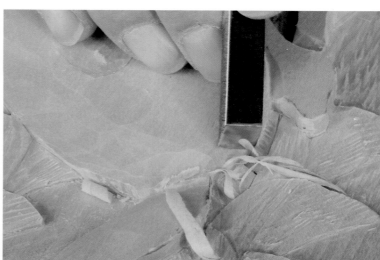

Shape the hindquarter.

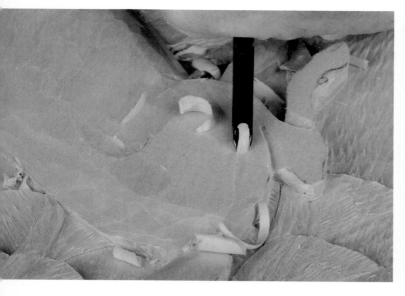

With the #11/4mm make a muscle cut parallel to the hind-quarter.

Shape the surface into the gouge cut you made for the muscle.

44

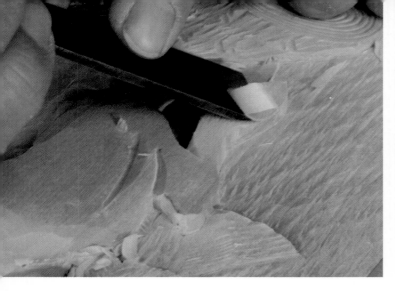

Use a #1/18 to take down the trailing edge of the leg using a tapered sliding cut.

With a sliding cut shape the leading edge of the upper leg.

Do the same thing on the trailing edge of the background leg.

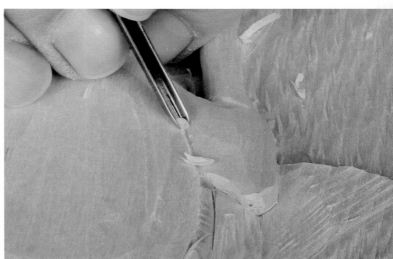

Soften the folds with a #11/2mm.

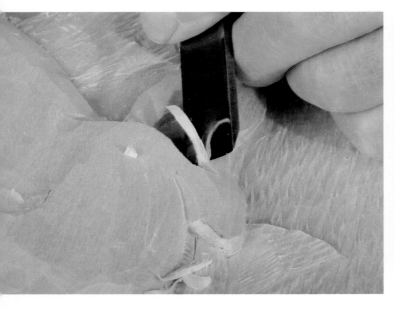

Bevel the leading edge of the leg.

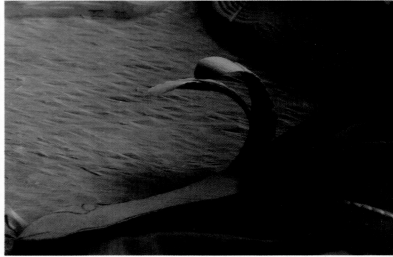

Start at the top of the front leg and shape the trailing edge. As you approach the knee bring your cut out, leaving the knee full.

Below the knee cut in again...

At the top of the leg that is in the background I need to come across at the top because I don't have access for a sliding cut.

continuing through the hoof.

Then I can shape the trailing edge as I did with the other legs.

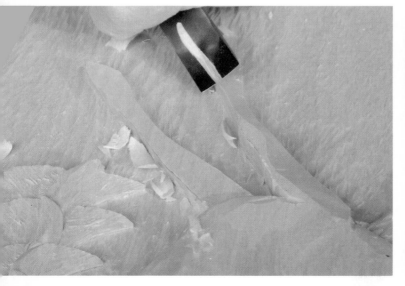

Bevel the leading edge of the leg, again coming out at the knee.

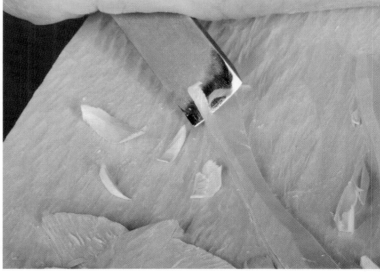

On these leading surfaces I make a little valley at the tops of the hooves...

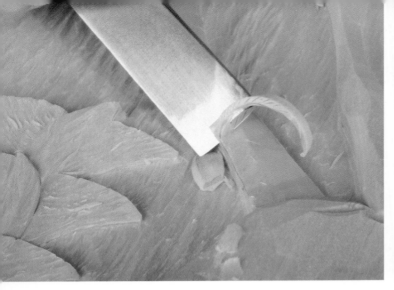

and flatten the cut at the knee joint.

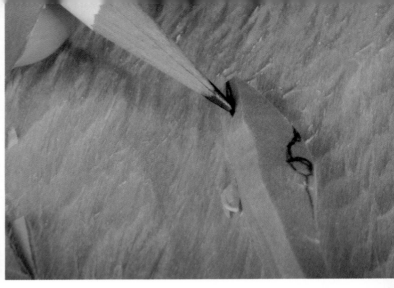

Mark center split in the hoof.

Square the tips of the hooves.

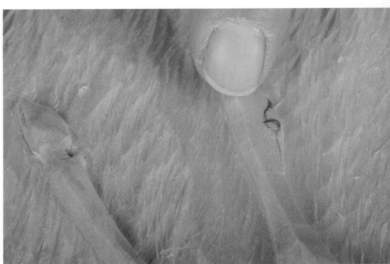

The shaping of the hoof is easier than you might think. You start at this indention above the hoof.

Redraw the back of the hooves and the dewclaws.

Cut across it with a #6/8mm...

stopping at the line of the dewclaw.

Switch to a #11/2mm and come over the dew claw...

Cut back the other way, across the front, going down to the background...

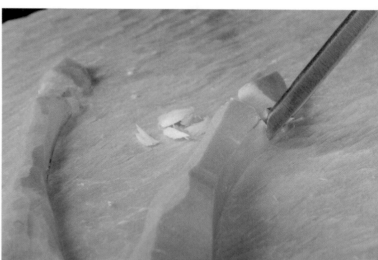

and down to the background, ending in an undercut.

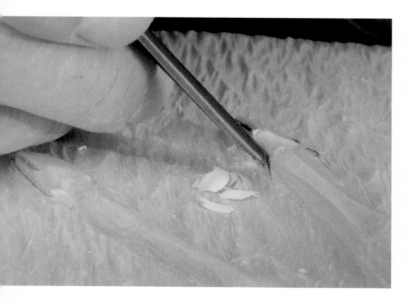

with an undercut.

Do the same on the underside of the dewclaw.

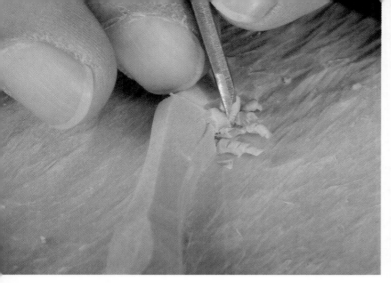

Use the #1/6mm to shape the dew claw.

Shape the hoof, rounding it back to the line of the split.

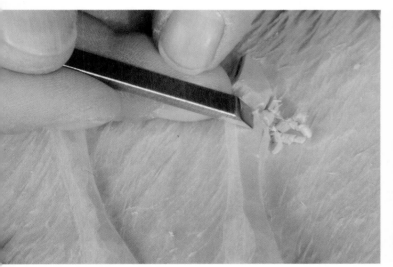

Use the same tool to shape the joint area. Undercut a little as you come to the background.

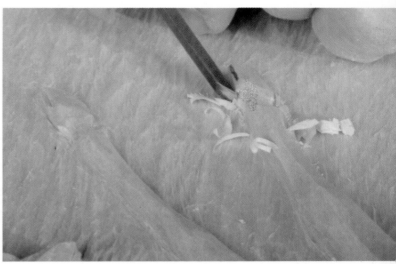

Do the same on the other side of the split, ending with a slight undercut.

Use a #11/4mm to cut the back of the hoof between it and the dewclaw. Be careful because it is very easy to break off the dewclaw.

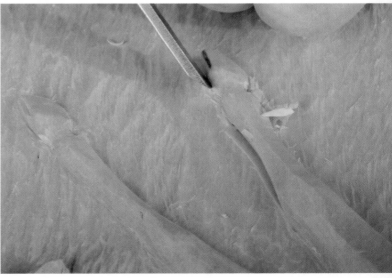

With a #1/12mm, undercut up to the knee...

49

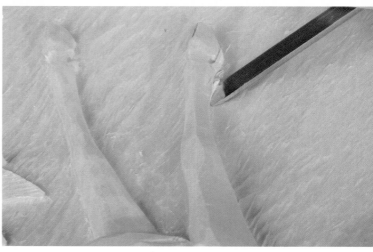

and from the knee to the chest. This brings out the shape of the knee.

Cut a groove along the back surface of the outer leg and down behind the knee to bring out the muscle.

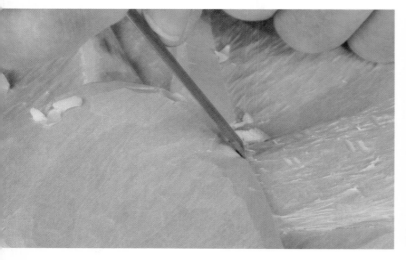

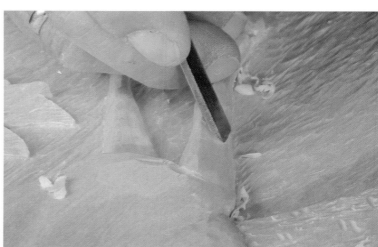

Shape the chest to bring out the upper leg.

Shape and blend the leg surface with the muscle.

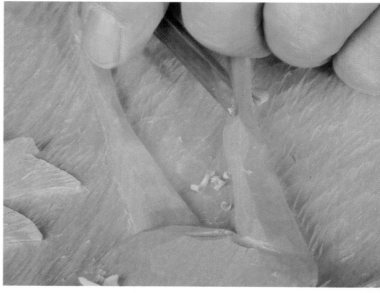

Continue the undercut on the back edge of the leg. You must be carefully not to go so deeply that you separate the leg from the background.

Continue to shape the leg.

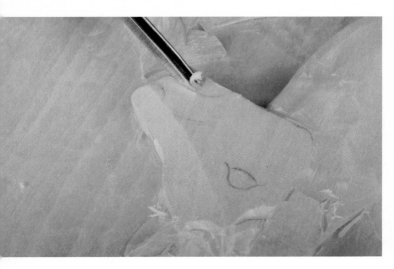

With a #11/2 cut the lines of the mouth...

Continue up the snout, then turn the tool over and round over the eye and back to the ear.

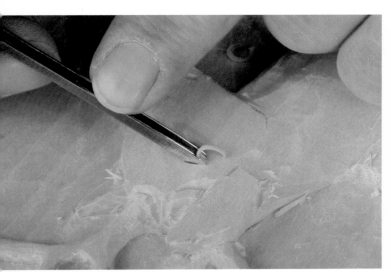

and the mouth.

Make a cut up the center of the forehead to the antlers.

With a #4/10mm shape the nose leaving a definite, but slight line at the top.

Cut around the eye...

back to the ear.

with the #4/18mm shape the area in front of the eye down to the jaw.

With the #6/18mm come under the eye and back to the ear.

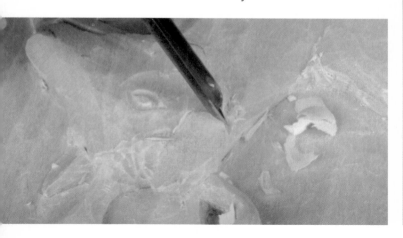

Cut across the base of the ear.

Shape the front of the lower jaw.

With a #1/6mm define the line of the mouth by taking it deeper.

Shape the face. When shaping I usually make a sliding cut...

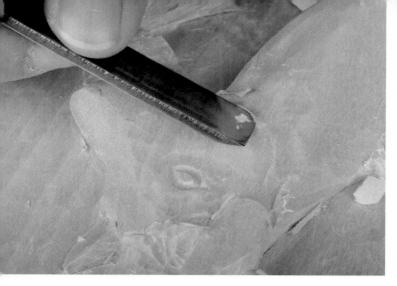

rolling the tool as I go.

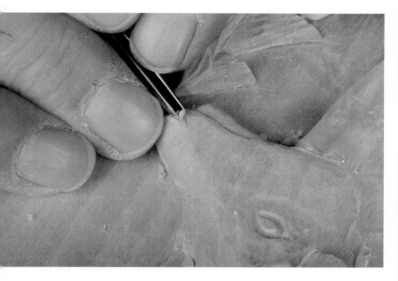

With a #11/2mm carve the nostrils. The motion is down and back up....

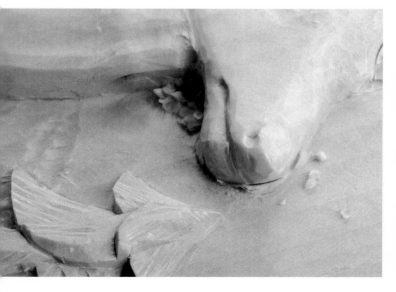

for this result.

To cut the line of the eye place a #4/6mm gouge in the corner and incise a line along the upper lid...

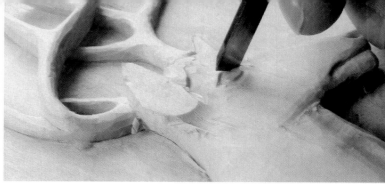

to the back corner.

Repeat along the lower margin of the eye.

The result. The cuts are not deep.

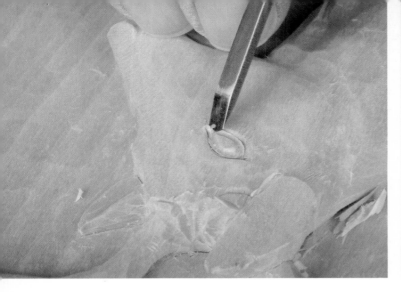

With a #2/4mm skew cut the corner.

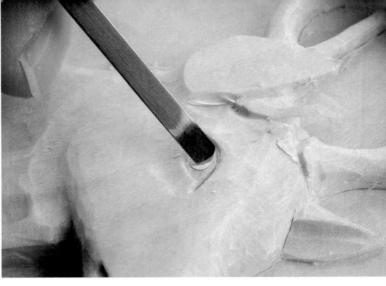

Shape it with the skew.

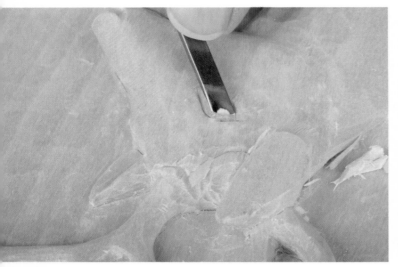

Shape the eye with the same tool.

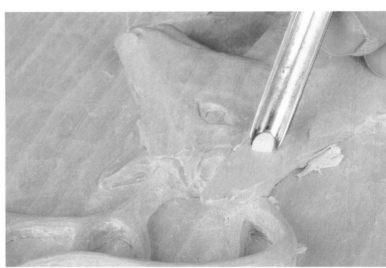

Open the ear with a #11/6mm working from the top and bottom to the middle.

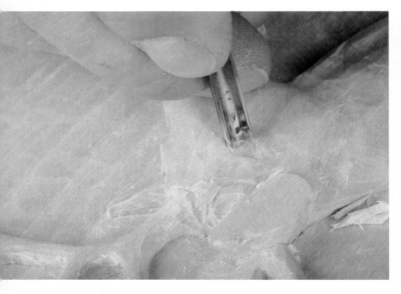

With light pressure use the #11/4mm to cut the line of the pupil.

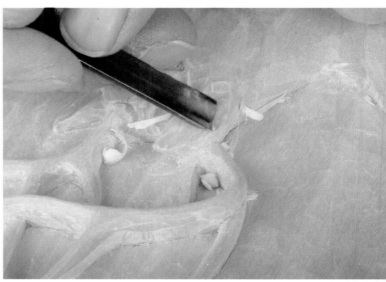

Shape and size the ear opening with the #4/10mm.

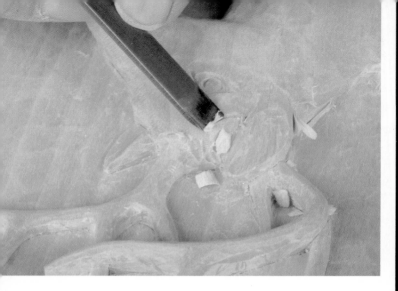

Clean up the forehead.

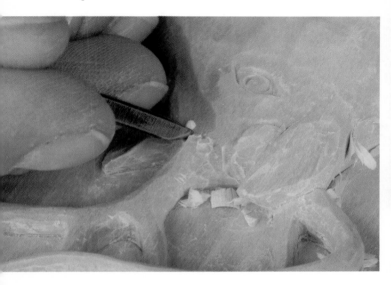

With a #11/2mm put some notches at the base of the antler, cleaning up the chips with a skew.

Outline the eyelids with a #11/1mm.

A final smoothing and we are ready to carve hair.

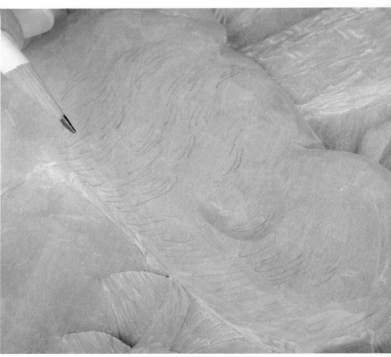

Draw the major patterns for the hair.

To make hair I use a #4/10mm. For the hair at the back I need to roll the tool. To do this I hold the edges of the tool between my thumb and forefinger and support it with the middle finger.

As I move down the body I change my hand position so the thumb is in front of the tool, in the concave cup.

The fingers are quite flat against the surface of the wood.

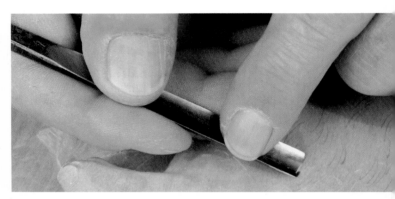

The tool is held very low. With a little pressure use the middle of the blade to cut in a shallow arc. This is the beginning...

I start the cut with the center of the blade...

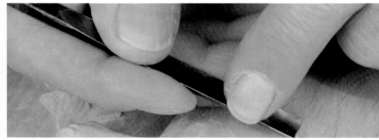

and this is the end. My left forefinger holds the blade, but does not add pressure to the cut. Be patient and take short, shallow cuts. If you hold the tool too far upright you will get a cut that is too deep.

and roll it to the left. This lifts out a thin short cut. The hair is formed by continuing this over the body, one cut after another.

To get in this depression I need to switch to a #6/8mm and work from the top.

On the neck the hair is longer so I use a #4/18 and cut a little deeper, while using the same technique.

The #4/18mm is also used on the tail.

Ready for staining.

Occasionally you may need to use an alternative hand position to get in certain spots.

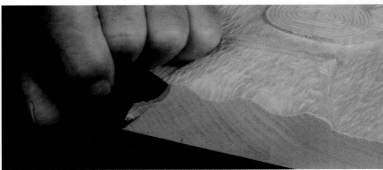

Take away the saw marks around the edges...

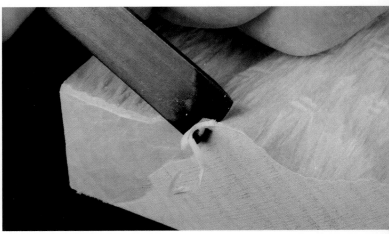

and add a slight bevel.

Staining

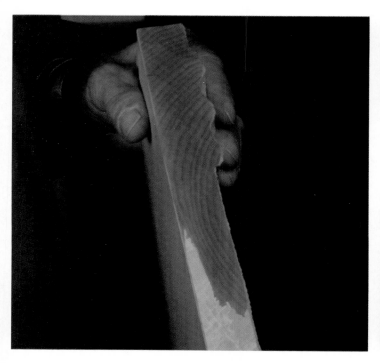

I use a water-based wax stain with ammonia. It works well on basswood, where oil stain gets spotty. I always start with the edges. I use two brushes one to apply the stain, and a dry brush to wipe away the excess. The first coat is a light, pear wood stain applied over the complete piece.

I do the sides and back and let them dry before doing the front.

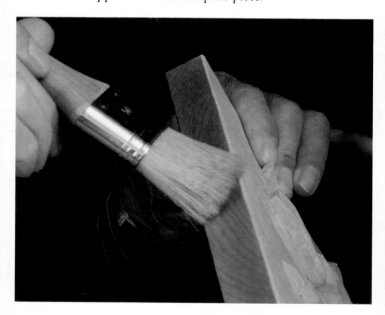

Use the dry brush almost immediately after applying the stain with the other brush. By wiping the stain away the finish is made even. Without this step the application would be spotty.

When the back is dry, turn the piece over and apply the stain one section at a time...

Brushing away the excess right after application.

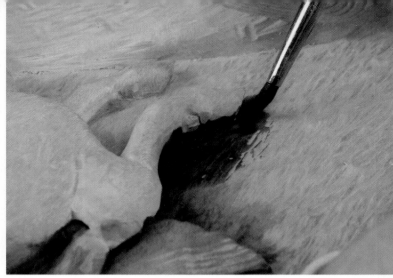

Where the figure is highly raised from the surface, come about halfway up the edge of the carving to add to the illusion of dimensionality.

When the color is even, the stain is dry enough to add some darker, light walnut stain for accent.

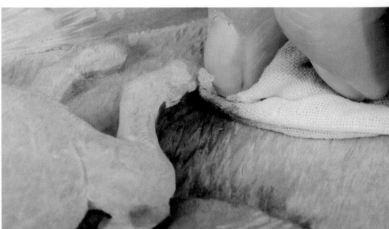

In the grass areas I need to use more water in my wiping rag, to get between the blades of grass.

I begin on the tail, leaving a light edge at the back. Immediately rub the stained area with a damp cloth to remove the excess and ensure a even finish.

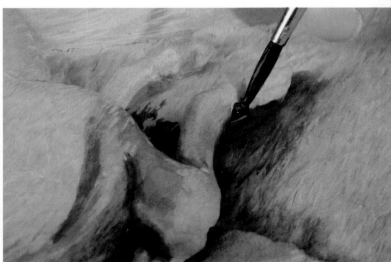

The hooves and dewclaws need to be darker, so I let the stain set longer before wiping.

Stain around the figures...

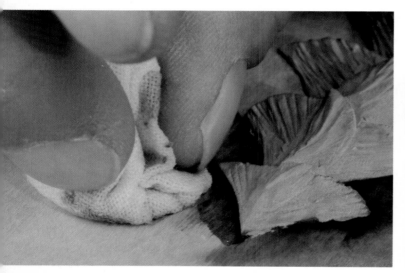

wiping the excess away with a damp cloth.

Do the same with the major cuts in the figures, like these middle boughs of the trees. This accentuates the carving.

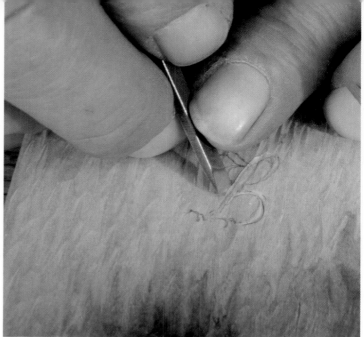

Sign your work.

Ready for polishing.

Polishing

When the stain has dried, polish the piece with a brush mounted on a power drill. I want it to be fairly slow, about 400 rpm.

In tighter areas this small brush gets in to do the details.

To protect the work I apply a white liquid wax. This particular wax is water and alcohol-proof. Apply with one brush...

When the wax is completely dry, buff it with the rotary brush. Be sure to use one without dark stain residue on it. This takes very little pressure.

and wipe it off with another. Brush in the direction of the grain or you may get some stroke marks.

Use the small straight brush to get into the tight spots.

The finished carving.